What's Down There?
Questions and Answers
About the Ocean

by Dinah Moché

SCHOLASTIC INC.

New York   Toronto   London   Auckland   Sydney

Cover photo: Animals Animals © R. Ingo Riepl.
Inside photos: U.S. Navy, pp. 6, 16, 19, 22, 28, 55; National Oceanic
and Atmospheric Administration, pp. 10, 31, 37, 39, 47;
Photo Researchers, p. 14—Ron Church, p. 33—V.B. Scheffer; Florida Department of
Commerce, pp. 19, 42; Nova Scotia Film Bureau, p. 25; Wide World/AP, pp. 26, 37, 51, 63;
Woods Hole Oceanographic Institution, p. 52; Lockheed Missiles & Space Co., p. 57;
UPI, p. 59; Mobil Oil Co., p. 60.

ISBN 0-590-42855-1

12 11 10 9 8 7 6 5 4 3 2   1 2 3 4 5 6/9

Printed in the U.S.A.   28

Contents

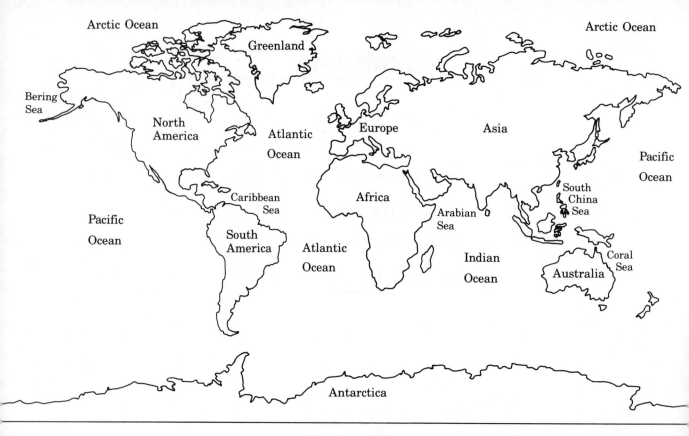

Map of the World

The Land and the Water

How many oceans are there?

There is only one ocean. It covers 71 percent of our Earth. There is enough water in the ocean to give every person in the world an Olympic-size swimming pool and have plenty left over.

Parts of the ocean have different names — Pacific, Atlantic, Indian, and Arctic. Some parts are called seas — the Caribbean, the Bering Sea, the Coral Sea. Ocean or sea, they are all connected, and you could sail around the world without ever touching land.

Where did the water come from?

Most of the water in the ocean came from inside the Earth.

When our planet formed almost 5 billion years ago, it had no ocean. The enormous hollow places on its rocky surface were practically dry. But a great quantity of water was trapped in the rocks.

Heat, given off by radioactive elements in the rocks, changed the water to steam. The steam escaped into the air through volcanoes and hot springs. (This is still going on today.) When the steam cooled, it changed back to water. Gradually this water filled the ocean.

Myojin Reef volcano, south of Japan, is part of the ring of active volcanoes (called the Ring of Fire) that stretches along the coastlines and islands of the Pacific Ocean.

How old is the ocean?

Today's ocean began to take shape about 200 million years ago. Scientists think that at one time our planet had only one supercontinent surrounded by water. Then the continent—called Pangaea, meaning "all earth"—broke into huge pieces that drifted apart.

Antarctica moved toward the South Pole. India crunched into Asia. North America inched away from Europe, and South America left Africa.

The continents are still drifting apart—about two inches a year. The Atlantic Ocean is getting wider, and the Pacific Ocean is shrinking.

Asia

North America

Europe

Africa

South America

India

Australia

Antarctica

Pangaea

225 Million Years Ago

What is it like on the bottom of the sea?

The ocean floor is made of rock. It has wide, flat areas, but it also has high mountains and steep valleys. The world's longest mountain range is in the ocean. Called the Mid-Oceanic Ridge, it winds through the Atlantic, Indian, and Pacific oceans for about 40,000 miles. The tallest peaks in the ridge stick out of the ocean as islands. Iceland is one of these mountain peaks.

Most of the rocky ocean floor is covered with sediment. Plant and animal remains as well as particles of matter from the land, the air, and outer space drift down endlessly. In a thousand years, this sediment piles up about one inch.

The drawing shows divers 108 feet below the surface, examining Cobb Seamount, an extinct volcano off the northwestern coast of the United States.

How deep is the ocean?

The average depth is about two miles.

As you go out to sea, the land slopes down gradually. In the waters closest to the shore, the submerged land is called the *continental shelf.* As it slants deeper, it is called the *continental slope.* At the very bottom are the great *ocean basins.*

The deepest known spot in the ocean is in a big valley called the Marianas Trench in the Pacific Ocean. It is nearly seven miles below the surface. The tallest mountain on land—Mount Everest, in Asia—is almost six miles high. If it were set in the Marianas Trench it would be completely covered by water.

Is it light or dark underwater?

The deeper you go underwater the darker it gets.

Sunshine lights the top of the ocean. But it doesn't go very deep because the water absorbs it. Even in very clear water there is never enough light to see below 1,000 feet.

Water offshore is often not clear. It may be totally dark just 50 feet down.

Is the ocean crowded with plants and animals?

Most of the ocean is practically deserted. All plants and most animals live in the upper waters—where the ocean is less than 600 feet deep.

The waters of the *continental shelves* are full of life. The seaweeds we use for food grow there, and most of the fish we eat come from these waters.

These tropical fish, corals, and spiny urchins are not in a fish bowl. They were photographed in the shallow waters off Hawaii.

The Deep Blue Sea

Why does the ocean look blue?

Water is colorless. The ocean looks blue in bright sunlight because the water scatters the *blue* rays in the light more than the other colors in sunlight.

If clouds cover the sun, the ocean looks gray. Tiny green or red plants and animals can make the ocean take on their colors. Mud colors the ocean brown or yellow. The clearer the water, the bluer the ocean looks.

The color and the surface of the ocean changes with weather conditions.

How hot does the ocean get?

Ocean water is heated by the sun. It gets hottest in the tropics where the sun shines most. It freezes when the temperature drops below 28° F. Ocean temperatures range from 28° F around the North and South Poles to 96° F in the Persian Gulf.

Because sunshine can't penetrate to deep water, the ocean gets colder as you go deeper. The temperature at the bottom of the ocean is below 37° F, even in the sunny tropics.

Seals in the icy Antarctic, and bathers on the warm sunny beaches of Florida.

Why is the ocean salty?

Most of the salt in the ocean is washed from the land by rain, then carried by rivers to the ocean. This adds about 4 billion tons of salt to the ocean every year.

Salt also comes from inside the Earth. Material containing salt flows up through the ocean floor. Underwater volcanoes hurl out still more.

The ocean is getting saltier all the time. Water bringing salt flows in. At the same time, water evaporates from the surface and leaves the salt behind.

What makes the ocean move?

Currents move water all around the world. Surface currents are powered mainly by winds. They move warm water from hot, sunny regions toward the North and South Poles. Subsurface currents move icy water away from the Poles.

Up and down currents occur when cold, heavier salt water sinks, and warm, lighter, less salty water rises.

Currents are important because they affect our weather, and because they carry food and oxygen for sea life.

How are underwater mountains formed?

Powerful volcanoes and earthquakes keep reshaping the land and the sea.

Over and over again, undersea volcanoes hurl fiery melted rock into the water, where it cools and hardens. New sea floor, mountains, and islands are built up.

Earthquakes occur when layers of rock on the ocean floor move suddenly. Old mountains are tumbled and new ones are pushed up.

A new island pushing up from the ocean floor in the Pacific.

Why is there high tide and low tide?

At the beach you can see the water move in over the sand and then go back out again twice a day. The regular rise and fall of the ocean about every 12 hours is called the *tide*. Daily tides are caused mainly by the force of the moon's gravity pulling on Earth.

The tides in the Bay of Fundy, between New Brunswick and Nova Scotia in Canada, are the highest in the world. Between low and high tide, the waters rise almost 44 feet. The waterline on this ship anchored near the bay shows the dramatic rise and fall of the tides.

What causes waves?

Most waves are caused by wind. If you blow across water in a pan, your breath makes ripples on the surface. When strong winds blow over thousands of miles of open ocean, they make waves.

Huge, destructive waves called *tsunamis* (Sue-NAH-mees) are created by underwater earthquakes, volcanoes, or landslides. These waves can rise over 100 feet near shore and crash with colossal force.

Tsunamis used to kill thousands of people on the coasts and islands of the Pacific Ocean. Today an international warning system alerts people in time to save lives.

Ships and houses in Kodiak, Alaska, suffered the destructive force of a tsunami. Tsunamis are also called tidal waves.

Animals and Plants

What kinds of animals live in the ocean?

Over 200,000 different kinds of animals have been found in the ocean. Besides fish, there are sponges, worms, insects, snakes, salamanders, and seals.

Sea animals fall into three groups. *Zooplankton*, the animals that float and drift with the current, range from the tiny microbes to the big jellyfish. *Nekton*, the good swimmers, include fish, turtles, and whales. *Benthos*, the animals that crawl or burrow on the ocean floor or attach themselves to the rocks, include shrimp, clams, snails, and coral.

The porpoise, or dolphin, is a small-toothed mammal. This one, called Tuffy, was trained by the U.S. Navy for underwater experiments.

What is the biggest animal?

The blue whale is the biggest animal that has ever lived on Earth. It is bigger than the dinosaurs. The largest blue whale ever recorded measured 110 feet.

Although they can only live in water to support their bulk, blue whales are mammals. They have lungs and must surface regularly to breathe air. Whales have backbones and are warm-blooded, and mother-whales feed their calves milk from their bodies.

These animals are endangered by whale hunters, who slaughter them for profit. Many nations fear the blue whales will become extinct and have agreed not to hunt them at all.

A blue whale blowing air through the blowhole on the top of its head. The warm air from the whale's lungs is filled with water vapor so it looks as if the whale is spouting water.

Blue Whale

How many kinds of fish are there in the ocean?

There are over 20,000 different kinds of fish. They come in a great variety of colors, shapes, and sizes.

All fish are cold-blooded. Most have a skeleton made of bone. They use fins for balancing, steering, and driving themselves through the water. Many fish have a protective covering of scales. As a fish gets older, new material is added to the outer edge of each scale, forming a growth ring. By counting these rings, you can tell the age of a fish.

Humpback, or pink, salmon are Pacific Ocean fish. Though they live most of their lives in the sea, the fish return to inland rivers to breed. Scientists believe they use their sense of smell and taste (of the waters) to find their way back to their breeding grounds.

How do fish breathe?

Fish need oxygen to live, just as land animals do. They have gills instead of lungs to get oxygen underwater.

To breathe, a fish opens its mouth and draws in water. The water has oxygen. It flows over the gills, which are behind the mouth. The gills absorb the oxygen from the water and release waste gases into the water. This waste water goes back into the ocean through openings on the sides of the fish's head. These openings are covered by movable flaps.

Can fish see and hear?

Most fish have big round eyes that see up, down, and sideways. They have no eyelids, so they sleep with their eyes open. Many fish have internal ears that hear squeaks, grunts, rumbles, and other ocean noises.

Fish can also smell, taste, and feel. They have a row of sensitive cells, called a *lateral line*, on each side of their body. This line allows them to sense moving objects in the water.

Which fish is the most dangerous?

The great white shark, nicknamed "the man-eater," has attacked the most people. Its powerful jaws hold rows of big, sharp, jagged teeth that can bite through bone. When a tooth wears away or is lost, a new one grows in its place.

These fish hunt other fish and swallow them whole. But when excited, they will attack anything in the water—even ships. A full-grown white shark can weigh 7,000 pounds and measure 40 feet long.

If it ever stopped swimming, a great white shark would die. It breathes by always keeping its mouth open and ramming water through its gills. So it has to swim even while it sleeps.

The great white shark is one of the most feared ocean animals. It is a fast swimmer and has jaws of terrifying, sawlike teeth. The white shark lives in warm ocean waters.

What do ocean animals eat?

Tiny plants called *phytoplankton* (FI-toe-plankton) are the basic food in the ocean. Billions and billions of these plants float on the surface of the water. They are eaten by the drifting animals called zooplankton. Then small fish and shellfish eat the zooplankton. Finally, bigger fish, sharks, and toothed whales eat the small fish and shellfish. This is called a food chain.

There are giant sightless worms, over six feet long, near the hot springs on the ocean bottom. These strange animals have no mouths or stomachs. They do not depend on plants. Instead, billions of bacteria live in the central part of their bodies. The bacteria use sulfur chemicals and heat from the hot springs to make food that energizes the worms.

Key Largo, off the southern tip of Florida, is the site of a national marine sanctuary, where plant and animal life is protected for future generations.

Are there lots of plants in the ocean?

More plants grow in the ocean than on land. But plants don't grow below 600 feet because it is too dark. Ocean plants use light from the sun to grow. They absorb water and nutrients from the ocean.

The most familiar ocean plants are the green, brown, red, and blue-green seaweeds that wash up on the beach.

The largest plant in the ocean is the Pacific giant kelp. It can grow a foot and a half in a single day. The largest kelp measures 196 feet, practically as long as an ice-hockey rink.

Can people eat ocean plants?

Seaweeds are used as food by millions of people. Extracts of seaweeds are used in ice cream, candies, jellies, medicines, and beer. People can eat phytoplankton, too, but there isn't any practical way to harvest them.

In Japan, seaweed and phytoplankton are grown near the coast and in ponds, and are harvested to feed people. Someday many countries may farm ocean plants to raise food for their growing populations.

You and the Ocean

How far down in the ocean have humans gone?

Nearly seven miles. Jacques Piccard and Donald Walsh made the deepest dive on record in 1960. It took their ship *Trieste* 4 hours and 48 minutes to get down to the ocean bottom in the Marianas Trench. The force pressing on their cabin was over 300 million pounds. Even there they saw a fish swim by.

There are more than 12,000 miles of beaches along the coastline of the United States. The entire shoreline of the United States totals almost 85,000 miles.

What special dangers are there for humans underwater?

Even a good swimmer cannot stay underwater very long without coming up for air. The deeper you go underwater, the harder the water presses on your body. At 1,000 feet, the force is over one million pounds. The air you breathe must be at the same pressure as the water around you or your body will be crushed.

A snorkel—a breathing tube that sticks up above the water—allows a swimmer to stay facedown just below the surface. To go deeper, a swimmer must carry a supply of air.

With a face mask and breathing tube (snorkel) extending up into the air, swimmers can breathe facedown in the water.

What is scuba diving?

Scuba diving is a way for a person to swim freely underwater. Scuba is short for self-contained underwater breathing apparatus.

Scuba divers strap tanks of air onto their backs. A connecting hose leads to a mouthpiece that the diver breathes through. When a diver breathes in, air flows through the tube. A regulator supplies the air at the right pressure to balance the crushing force of the water. When the diver breathes out, the air stops flowing. Used air goes bubbling into the ocean.

A scuba diver also wears a face mask to see clearly underwater, and a wet suit to stay warm in cold water. The suit traps a layer of water next to the body. The water, heated by the diver's body, keeps out the cold.

A scuba diver carries tanks of air for breathing underwater. Scuba divers can go far below the surface of the water.

What are the bends?

A serious illness that divers get when they rise to the surface too fast.

When divers breathe high-pressure air, the extra air dissolves in their bodies. They can breathe it out normally if they surface slowly. But if they rise too fast, the quick drop in the outside pressure produces gas bubbles in their blood. These bubbles block normal blood flow, causing pain, paralysis, and sometimes even death.

Can robots work underwater?

Yes. Robots, unmanned submersibles, do jobs that are simple or too dangerous for humans. They have mechanical arms and claws to dig trenches, lay pipeline, recover trial torpedos after tests, and pick up salvage from shipwrecks. Robots have cameras for "eyes" to inspect equipment and underwater oil fields.

How does a deep diving suit work?

Deep diving suits must protect divers from great water pressure and cold. They cover a diver's whole body and have cables for air supply and communication.

One type of suit, made of synthetic rubber, keeps air inside the suit at the same pressure as the surrounding water. Another type of suit is made of sealed metal or plastic. This tough material protects a diver the same way the hull of a submarine protects its crew. The air inside the suit is always at the same pressure as the air at the surface, so divers can rise to the surface quickly without getting the bends.

A marine botanist working deep under water in a specially designed deep diving suit called a Jim suit.

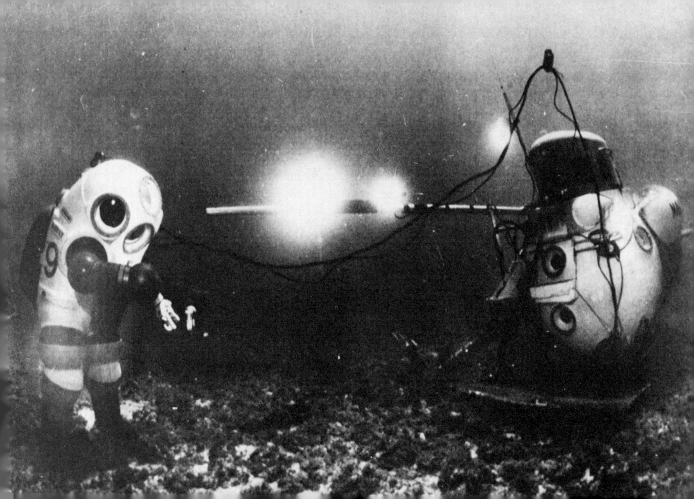

Which ships dive underwater?

Submarines, submersibles, and bathyscaphes can go underwater. Their hulls are built strong enough to withstand deep-water pressure. The air, pressure, and temperature inside the ships are kept at the same level as on land.

Submarines are large craft used mainly by the military for defense. They have ballast tanks for diving and surfacing. To go down, the tanks are filled with water. To surface, the tanks are emptied.

Submersibles are small submarines. They are used to explore and work on the ocean bottom at depths of a few miles for several hours. A bathyscaphe is a submersible used for deep-sea exploration.

The Alvin *is a submersible, a small submarine. It is used by the Woods Hole Oceanographic Institution on Cape Cod, Massachusetts, for deep sea research.*

What ship goes the deepest?

Bathyscaphes go down to the deepest parts of the ocean, but they don't travel much along the bottom. A bathyscaphe has a small, round steel cabin for the crew, which is joined to a big float. Some tanks in the float are filled with gasoline, which is lighter than water, to keep the ship afloat. Others are ballast tanks. The ship sinks by flooding the ballast tanks with water. It rises by emptying the tanks and dropping metal weights.

The bathyscaphe Trieste *was designed by Auguste Piccard and his son Jacques. Bathyscaphes go down to the ocean floor. The* Trieste *has made the deepest ocean dive.*

How do ships navigate underwater?

Sonar (<u>so</u>und <u>na</u>vigation and <u>r</u>anging) is a device that uses sound waves to locate objects underwater.

Sound travels better in water than in air. When sound is beamed out, it hits an object, and an echo returns. Computers can turn the echoes into pictures and tell how far away an object is.

Sonar is used not only to navigate submarines but also to locate fish, find shipwrecks, and map undersea mountains and valleys in the total darkness of the deep.

Pilots at the controls of the research submarine Deep Quest *built by the Lockheed Company for ocean research.*

Will the ocean ever run out of fish?

The answer depends on what humans do. Pollution kills plants and animals. To protect sea life, we must keep the ocean clean.

The world's fishermen catch over 150 billion pounds of fish and shellfish every year. People eat about half that amount. The rest is used for animal food, fertilizer, and fish oil.

Popular fish like tuna, flounder, herring, and cod are disappearing. They are killed before they breed and have young. To save the fish supply, countries can limit their catch. They can also breed fish on farms instead of relying solely on the ocean.

We now eat only about 500 of the more than 20,000 kinds of fish in the ocean. We can learn to eat other kinds of fish that are just as nourishing.

After months at sea, a whaling ship heads home with a catch of whales in tow. To conserve ocean life, many countries are limiting their catches of whales and fish.

Is there much oil under the ocean?

Over a quarter of the world's oil is under the ocean. It formed several hundred million years ago from tiny plants and animals that lived, died, and were buried deep in underwater mud. Very slowly their remains changed to oil, and the mud hardened into rock. The heavy rock squeezed the oil upward into pools.

Getting the oil out of the ocean is difficult. Deep and stormy water can kill workers and smash equipment. Every job must be done carefully to avoid oil spills that kill sea plants and animals.

Helicopters and boats bring workers and supplies to offshore oil fields. Pipelines and tankers carry the oil to shore.

An offshore oil platform in the North Sea. Countries around the world are searching for offshore oil as land reserves run out.

Will people live underwater some day?

It is possible to do that now. Researchers have developed sea-floor habitats—underwater dwellings—where people can live and work in a dry environment.

The air pressure inside a habitat is kept equal to the water pressure outside. When a diver enters a habitat through the hatch, the air inside keeps the water from rushing in. Because the air pressure inside is the same as the pressure outside, a diver can change quickly from a water environment to a dry environment without suffering any ill effects.

Divers enter NASA's Tektite II habitat some 50 feet below the surface. Such underwater "homes" provide scientists and engineers with the chance to live for long periods of time underwater to study the ocean.

How valuable is the ocean?

There are raw materials worth trillions of dollars in the ocean. When the salt is taken out, the water itself is valuable for drinking. The plant and animal life is a rich source of food.

Ocean water has over 100 million trillion pounds of dissolved minerals. Salt is just one of the minerals we get out of the ocean now. The ocean bottom has a wealth of oil, gas, coal, diamonds, and precious metals. It is estimated that there is more gold in the ocean than in all the banks in the world. If nations cooperate, the ocean's treasures can be used for everyone.